The Pisces

Michael Tavon

The Pisces

The Pisces

Poems
Quote,
Illustrations,
&
Lyrics

By Michael Tavon

Michael Tavon

Other Works

Poetry Collections

Nirvana: Pieces of Self-Healing vol 1
Nirvana: Pieces of Self-Healing vol.2
A Day Without Sun
Songs for Each Mood
Don't Wait 'Til I Die to Love Me
Dreaming in a Perfect World

Fiction Novels

God is a Woman
Far from Heaven

Affirmations and Quotes
Heal, Inspire, Love w/ Moonsouldchild
Self-Talks w/ Moonsoulchild

The Pisces

Amazon Self-Publishing
Kindle Direct Publishing

© 2021 by Michael Tavon
All rights reserved, including the rights to reproduce this book or portions thereof in any form whatsoever.

All contents are original works by author Michael Tavon, any redistribution without the author's consent illegal

Posting any content from this book without crediting the author is considered plagiarism.

Art cover design by Nick Davis

Michael Tavon

Author's Social Media:

Twitter: MichaelTavon
Instagram: @michaeltavonpoetry
TikTok: MichaelTavonPoetry

Cover Artist:

Instagram: NDArtlife
Facebook: NDArtlife by Nick Davis
Website: www.NDartlife.com

The Pisces

Note to Reader

For the best reading experience read the poems or sections in the order you're most drawn to by referring to the table of contents. Hopefully, this method will create a deeper emotional connection with the poems.

Michael Tavon

T.O.C

Part I: The Silver Lining...9
Part II: Rain & Dark Clouds...104
Part III: Star Gazing...142
Part IV: Constellations & Everything in Between...167

Michael Tavon

I:

The Silver Lining

Michael Tavon

Cloud Dreamer

My head remains
in the clouds
Because my dreams
keep me alive

The Pisces

Dear Pisces:

Stop looking into the future; it doesn't exist. Today, this present moment is the only blessing guaranteed. Soak in the love. Open your eyes to the light. The more you reach for the future that seems too elusive to grab, the more misery you'll bring to your beautiful heart. Appreciate every step you take. The present is a present, cherish it, or you will look back on your journey with miles of regret for overlooking everything you had in front of you.

Michael Tavon

People like You

People like you are stronger than given credit for. You bend over backwards for people who step over you, but spreading joy still comes more naturally than breathing. The world uses your kindness as a crutch to support their dead weight, but you don't let them break you. Despite being everyone's favorite afterthought, you never hesitate to save a loved one from their misery. You find reasons to smile with a heart permanently scarred and bruised. People like you have infinite reasons to become heartless, but you're stronger than the environment around you. Love conquers all, and you've defeated all odds. You're stronger than what you're given credit for. Never forget that.

Prison

I served my heart
the greatest justice
by releasing it from
the grudges
it was wrongly
imprisoned by

Michael Tavon

R.I.P to the old me

Rest in peace to the soul I used to know. You fought and clawed until you no longer recognized who you were; that's something to be proud of. At times you were lost, but you were always brave enough to follow your heart. Tears constantly flooded your eyes because you convinced yourself your heart was impossible to fall for. Your hope was a rollercoaster because you never felt confident enough to believe in yourself. Now that you're gone, you'd be happy to know, you've found someone who is proud to hold you at night, and your heart beats a mile a minute for them too. The dreams that once kept you up at night are now your reality. You no longer pour poison down your throat, to numb your sorrows. You no longer burn enough trees to kill a forest. Nor do you indulge in porn until your eyes sore. Now, you only enjoy those things in moderation. You should be proud you made it this far; now I'll take it from here Sorry I must let you go, you are now allowed to rest knowing all the work you put in didn't go in vain, without you I wouldn't be who I am today.

Note to Self:

"You are closer to the beginning than the end. When you view life from this perspective, you'll see there's no need to rush through anything. Each day is an opportunity to start fresh or move forward."

Michael Tavon

Conversations with my Imaginary Therapist

When I walk into the warm room
Decorated with pictures.
and degrees,
I stretch across the
Nude-colored chaise,

The therapist:
What brings you in today?

I'll take a deep breath
To allow my boiling
Nerves to settle
Like water on the stove
When the temperature is lowered

And say:

Some nights,
my bed might as well
Be a pallet of bricks
For how hard it is
To sleep with
So much self-pity
weighing down
on my aching back
I feel like I've failed
at everything in life
And what I protect
Wouldn't give a fuck
If I got hit by a truck
Because dying in my prime

The Pisces

Is what I fear most
What if people forget about me
Soon after I'm gone?
What if people decide
to admire me out of guilt
For not appreciating
me while I was here

The therapist jots some notes
And ask:

Why do you feel like this?

My response:

See, when you give
 so much of yourself
And receive little in return,
Your mind begins to wonder
If you're good enough

Therapist: so, you doubt yourself?

Me: (laughing)

If self-doubt were a drug
I would've relapsed a thousand times
I believe in myself,
But

Therapist: but what?

Me: sometimes it's like

Michael Tavon

My confidence is tiptoeing on
A tight rope,
I love myself,
But I fear the world
Doesn't appreciate me
Enough to catch me
When I fall

Therapist:

so, you don't trust the universe?

Me:

that's not it,
I just want to know
when will my time arrive?
Will I be alive to see it?

Therapist:
Before, you said
you feel like a failure, elaborate?

Me:
sometimes I feel like
I've put all my eggs
In one basket
But they cracked before
 I made it to my destination

I'm just exhausted from
Trying to balance
two separate lives

The Pisces

On a tightrope
While blindfolded

I just want the break I deserve
I just want that respect
I've worked so hard to earn

Therapist:

See you're an interesting mind
You're confident enough to create
And bold enough to love
But your happiness seems
to be predicated upon
Peer validation
And monetary value

I look away
and shake my head in denial
As the therapist continues
to pick me apart
cotton plants in slave hands

Therapist continues:

You let insecurities
Swallow you whole
Until you're so knee-deep in pity
You can't see how blessed you are?

Let go of the expectations
of how people should react
or feel about you,
and solely create for yourself.

Michael Tavon

If you're passionate
about what you do your joy
should never wither away
based on how you're perceived.
That's just my two cents.

I nod my head and say
"Damn, you could be right"

Searching for Myself

Let me discover myself
Without judging my path
I will make mistakes,
I will burn and crash
The flames won't last
 I will learn from the past,
 Rise above the rubble and ash,

My life is not for you
to understand
I'm afraid, I am brave
But this space,
I won't stay
–
I will move on, to grow

Side eyed stares -
 Stones, you may cast
I'm not built like you
My heart's not glass

You won't break me,
Project your fears
I don't need you here
Be like magic, disappear

I'm searching for myself -
I will get lost along the way

Michael Tavon

The old me is gone
I won't beg you to stay
I am strong enough
To roam alone
Within my soul,
I will find a new home

The Pisces

Make Peace

Make peace
with your past
Before you move on,
it will drag you
back down
If you don't

Michael Tavon

The Cult

Shame and Regret
Are the leaders
Of a cult called addiction

They lure their members
in with the promises
Of comfort and healing

Feeding poor
Young souls
Quick fixes
To soothe
Their traumas

they watch
with pleasure
as their pupils
fail to
sow their wounds
with alcohol and bandages

Shame and Regret
are the leaders of a cult
that will spit on you
when you've hit rock bottom

The Pisces

Choices

I could lose myself
In yesterday's thoughts
Or find new life
In the memories waiting
To be made today
I think I'm ready
to smile again

Healing is Uncomfortable

A thousand yesterdays held
captive inside the brick walls in
your mind, too stubborn to let
go, you've found comfort in
grief. Your future would have
only been a mile away if you had
stopped running backwards. You
cry to the sky for the clouds to
pour drops of solace, while
you're the one holding yourself
back. You live in hell's comfort
inn, cuz moving on seems
frightening to you.

When will you understand,
healing will not meet you in the comfort zone.
Growth only happens when you're ready to find
a new home outside of the miserable yesterday's
that reside in your mind.

<u>Shift</u>

Once you release
your mind from
The doubt
it's been caged in
you'll discover
the most beautiful joy
you will ever feel
and your reality will slowly
begin to shift
into the life
destined for you.

Michael Tavon

Floating

I'll reach for the sun
As long as my arms
can stretch wide
With passion and pride
by my side
Dead egos and silent hate
Won't make me cry, again

These wings were made to fly
High in a friendly sky.
I see the light
And I'm not afraid
 to soar above
the clouds now

Deadweight
won't keep me down
I'll float lightly over the clouds

Float
Soar
Ascend...
to my dreams

I can see clearly now
And I believe wholeheartedly

Waterchild

Ocean, how do
You always feel like home
When I feel off-course
You tell me to go with the flow

Cool and warm
You welcome me
with open arms
Despite how long
I was gone

Safe in your presence
Free of Yesterday's harm
Saltwater healing
You soothe my emotional scars

When I believe
I'm 'Bout to drown
to a deep demise
Your waves carry my body
'til the sun swells my eyes

You taught me
how to be strong and gentle
For my mental
You want me for me
despite my issues

Michael Tavon

Ocean,
You taught me
how to be calm
Amid heavy storms

You said,
No matter where
I roam
I'll never be alone

'Cause of you
I no longer
Detest my darkness
When I reflect and see
Not all-night skies are starless

Just like you,
The world may be too afraid
To explore the deep dark depths
Beyond my surface
But it doesn't
make me worthless
If passion
Swims deeply inside me
I have purpose

Thank you for always
Being by my side
Forever your waterchild

In Search Of…

You've spent a lifetime searching for love in homes that never welcome your light. You constantly try to break through walls that were created to push you away. You allow others to make a home out of you rent-free, because your heart falls so hard you believe everyone you love will protect your heart from breaking. When they inevitably pack their coat and never come back you rush to find the next resident to fill the vacancy. Your fear of being alone has created a place in your heart that only feels worthy when someone decides to visit for small pockets of time. You have yet to realize you already possess all the love you need. Be your own home. Appreciate the blissful space that resides inside you. Find solace in solitude.

Self-love

Sometimes I smile and sing
into the mirror
To remind me
How beautiful I am

When I'm not plucking
Grey hairs
Or tracing the wrinkles
In my skin
The mirror is my best friend

I stare into the glass
Like it's an endless realm
And chant positive affirmations
To Myself

My young naked soul
loved in whole
The way it deserves
My young naked soul
Doesn't hurt anymore

Building a Fire

I have a problem with not saying what's on my mind. I'm awful at being straightforward but a master at being passive-aggressive. Expressing what bothers me feels like a death sentence to the connections I value. I allow tiny fires to burn inside my heart until enough fuel creates an explosion. My fear of upsetting people results in a thousand flames burning inside me. I must understand some bridges are worth burning when it comes to protecting my peace.

Michael Tavon

Tired of Trying

My heart was exhausted
after chasing behind
People who got a rush
out of turning their back on me.
I would sprint to their aid
whenever they called
but when I was falling apart
they never provided
a shoulder to lean on,
so I stood all alone.
Excuses were the second language
they spoke fluently
whenever I reached out for help.
Loyalty was a home
That became foreign to them

I grew tired of giving
The best of me
To people
Who was committed
to disappointing me

I became fatigued of
Moving mountains for people
who would barely
 lift a finger for me

Deep down

The Pisces

I knew it was
time to move on
Somehow, they always
found a way to take advantage
Of my compassion

By using my strength
against me

Eventually, I realized
When it was time to
pack up my heart,
~and find a home
where its loyalty
would be appreciated

Michael Tavon

Gentle Reminder:

"Don't hold grudges. They're heavy on the heart and they only weigh you down."

Dear Pisces II:

The universe inside you is ready to be explored, so dream infinitely. Your imagination is a superpower, your sensitivity is a gift. With those you intuitively possess the ability to manifest the life you desire but don't get so high in the clouds that you lose the ground of reality. Remember the journey is a marathon, so pace yourself. Balance is key to unlocking your magic.

Michael Tavon

I Can Feel It

A change is gonna come
Rivers will flow in my direction
The Winds will carry me
to a beautiful fate

A change is gonna come
My heart will beat softly
My mind will release all doubt

A change is gonna come
I feel it in my bones
I feel it in my soul

A change is gonna come
Nothing will hold me back
I'm far stronger
Than any force that
Tries to block my blessings

A change is gonna come
I hear in the distance
I see it from afar

It's already mine to own,
It's ready to be held
In my palms

Greater Days

Today will be a great
and beautiful day,
I owe it to myself.

The sun rays will
Kiss my skin
The wind will carry me
Away from any element
That tries to bury me

I will soak in my blessings
Til the tan lines show

I will react less
to the negative forces
that try to penetrate my zen

I can't control my surrounding
But I am the master of my joy

Nothing will have the power
 to ruin my day

I am the master of my fate
And I say,
Love is my light
I will have a great
and beautiful day

Phobias

I understand,
the fear of flying
Or the anxious feeling
Some may get
When an eight-legged critter
Crawls on their skin
I,
Get stage fright
in public restrooms
So, I completely
Understand irrational fears
But what I can't fathom
Is a human
Fearing
or gaslighting
A burning hatred for
Another human
For simply being
In their own skin

The Pisces

Tag, You're It

O how our youthful
imaginations
Made the most mundane
Things
Seem like
Illustrious adventures

At what age did we
Stop looking at the clouds?

When did we become too old
To hide behind trees?

When did
the ice cream truck
Become unworthy to chase?

Summers stopped feeling
As warm as they used to
The moment adulthood blues
Robbed us of our youthful
essence

Michael Tavon

Group Home Stories

As a (former) group
home caretaker
I see life from a different angle
40 hours a week

The residents,
Two are toddlers trapped
In crippled adult bodies
One is blind, autistic,
And riddled with anxiety
Her best friend
Who she has minimal conversation
with has borderline
personality disorder
The other,
Has a mind rotting by the day,
With body more stubborn
Than a Republican,
The last resident
Has severe autism with cerebral palsy

Their behaviors
Consist of
Drooling,
Spitting
Shitting like elephants
Screaming loud enough

The Pisces

For the cops to be called,
Because one hates getting
her soiled diaper changed.
The howling
Floor stomping
And head-banging
When they don't get their way,
Leaning awkwardly mindlessly,
Seizures
And
Calling the staff niggers
incapable of counting to ten
But can say nigger
With conviction

All are incapable
of forming a sentence
So learning their
way of communication
Was imperative

After working here for
I've realized how
many blessings
 I've taken for granted
These precious beings
As pure as they are
Don't have the ability
To think for themselves
Or wipe their ass

Michael Tavon

Sometimes,
I check my own privilege
And feel ashamed
for complaining
things that don't matter

Where I'm From

Where I'm from
More names get written
in tombstones
Than degrees
As the temperature rises
Blood boils,
From fuming rage
Bullets fly south
Like a flock of cranes,
Forcing souls
 to find new domains
As lifeless bodies,
Rot in graves

Where I'm from
Grief pours
Like rain
From a mother's pain
As they bear witness to
their children
Getting fitted for caskets before
cap and gowns
Just sad songs
No graduation get downs
Just another
word heard around town

Michael Tavon

Where I'm from
Drugs get planted like seeds
Children fly high
Off strange leaves
Before they learn
To read

Where I'm from
pills are like skittles,
When you need a fix,
Treat your nose to some
Booger sugar
They remind us of pixy Stix
'Cuz Just like candy,
Drugs ain't hard to get,
Sad Young souls
Dying to get high

Many sad days
In the heat of June
Too many
Sudden goodbyes.
Too many gone too soons

So don't judge
If you not where I'm from,
We try hard to find affection,
Lost in a world
Where we've been
Beaten and neglected

Magic

Your existence
 is far from one dimension
Your soul bare layers
Too complex for the naked
Eye to capture
At a glance,
With a heart that beats
To the rhythm of jazz
And a smile warm enough
To make snow melt

Your purpose expands wider
Than your trauma and suffering
You're not defined by the pain
You are strong
You are faith personified

Not defined by cliches
and stereotypes
You are the architect
of your reality
By breaking down the barriers
Society tried to cage you in
You are more than what anyone
thought of

You took the little
You were given

Michael Tavon

Then created a land of color
And abundance
That's what I magic,
The magic
That lives inside you

Note to Self:

"While praising the light for all its glory don't neglect to appreciate the strength and wisdom you acquired while traversing through the darkness."

Michael Tavon

My Mind is a Haven

Affirm:

My mind is a safe space
to escape
when the world
is in retrograde.
When turbulent thoughts
 land on the surface
of my brain,
I control
what comes and goes.
Unwanted visitors may overstay,
ultimately, I control
The ideas that live inside me.
I will,
Choose the thoughts
that make me feel adorned,
welcomed and celebrated.
I will never
feel like a stranger
 in your own mind, again.

Comfort Zone Penitentiary

Your mind is a haven, but you treat it like a prison by caging your potential behind metal bars for committing the crime of not pursuing your dreams. You've allowed doubt to shackle your hands and feet because not trying feels safer than failing. You've imprisoned yourself behind your own comfort zone, where you will slowly die unfulfilled and alone if you never cultivate the strength to find a new home.

The Compass

When the light inside you
goes dim
And the journey becomes
Too dark to see
Remember your heart
Is the compass
That will guide you
To the path
Meant for you,
Allow your intuition
to lead you
You'll discover
Your purpose eventually

Alone is Wholeness

Alone, I stand
I don't mind
Aloneness is wholeness
I've eased the war
Ragin in my mind
At peace
With being a one-man band
At peace
With being the one
People refuse to understand
I innerstand higher
When no one is around
To pull me down
I became king
Of my temple
When independence
Was found

Michael Tavon

Note to Self:

"It takes a great deal of strength to finally let go of the emotional dead weight that's been keeping your heart heavy, but you got this."

Smile I

We often overlook the simplistic beauty of a smile. How could something so simple have such a lasting impact on our day? Many of us choose not to use our most beautiful asset. Maybe the world has conditioned us not to trust any smile because twisted souls hide their wicked intentions behind bright smiles all the time. I hope, you are strong enough to not let this gloomy world turn you cold. We need warmth. The world needs you to smile more.

Michael Tavon

Dark Matter

When dark thoughts
Linger like echoes,
It's time to
Close your eyes,
Inhale serenity,
Exhale fear,
And Begin
the cleansing process
Remember,
Your mind can only hold
So much weight
before breaking down
Release the stress
While you still possess
the strength
To love yourself

The Pisces

"Make sure you live before you actually die. Don't allow fear to hold you hostage in your comfort zone. Believe you're enough to step into the unknown. "

Michael Tavon

<u>Clutter</u>

Impulsive fear-based decisions
Will lead to a thousand
'what if's"
Flooding your thoughts.
Be fueled by faith,
so even if you fall short
Regret will not
clutter your mind

Drug Dealers Make More $$$ Than Poets

Sad truth is
People chase
The high
the numb
The lines
The dumb
The fix
The fun
The mix
The blunts
The tricks
The guns
The hits
The slugs
The shits
The rush
All to their blood

Yet run from

The healing
The love
The feeling
The sun
The seeking
The truth
The passion
The youth
The labor
The fruit
The acre

Michael Tavon

The bloom
The savior
The school

Sending Rsvp's
to their coffin
dying by toxins

Quick to buy a slow death
too poor to
Invest in mental health

Dear Pisces III

Why do you overthink
so often that
You fail to acknowledge
The ethereal power you possess?

Why do you
stack bricks of self-doubt
so high
Until you're unable
to see the beauty
On the other side
Of the walls you build?

Why do you bite your
tongue
to swallow your truth?
Why would you rather
hurt yourself
Than to tell others
how you truly feel?

why do you try to
escape reality
When life doesn't go your way,

Michael Tavon

When will you realize,
No matter how far you run
Your problems will
Remain attached
Like a shadow

The Pisces

"Never let their insecurities stop you from being proud of yourself. They only try to 'humble' you when your glow is too bright for them."

Michael Tavon

"Your life isn't supposed to make sense to anyone but you. Never live under anyone else's umbrella, you'll get rained on every time. Create your own expectations."

My life, Not Yours

My happiness
is not for you
to understand
I don't have to
Explain
If my dreams
Seem far fetched
Maybe you're
the one to blame

My shoes,
Don't fit your feet
We walk different paths
Keep the negativity
Your opinion,
I never asked

If you can't be proud
Of how far I've come
Marching down my own road
Keep your mouth closed
Stay in your comfort zone

My happiness,
Is not up for debate,
Remember this,
before you argue
With the decisions
I make

Racing to the Future

I chase the future
While racing
The past
hoping to meet
happiness at the finish line
Instead of taking it
one day at a time
I try to find shortcuts
To the finish line,
        The finish line,
      More struggle I find
      When I cut corners
      Shortcuts lead to deadends
      Deadends lead to starting over

I chase the future
'Til my knees sore
'Til my ankles swell
'Til my lungs no longer inhale
Then I find myself back
To where I began

distance never seems to close
Between me and the finish line
No matter how hard I try

The Pisces

Maybe,
I should take my time
Appreciate the strides
 I make toward
The finish line

Enjoy the blessings
I have today

The past is my wisdom
The present is my gift
I need to realize this soon,
obsessing over the finish line
Is destroying my health

It's okay to have goals
It's fine to aspire
To win the race
But
What good is a win
If I don't appreciate
the hardships
It endured to make it

Michael Tavon

Hip-Hop Raised Me II

Common taught me
how to love women
LL taught me
How to appreciate them more
Too short told me
to never trust a bitch
Snoop said we don't love them hoes

Ice Cube said fuck the police
Even on good days
Hov said own my masters
Never be a slave

Lupe said don't be
another dumb nigga
surviving off food and liquor

Yeezy taught me how
To be a college dropout
And still touch the sky
While staying fly

Weezy taught me
To never be stagnant
be consistent, Practice
Take risks,
master my craft

'Pac taught me

The Pisces

the power of duality,
As long as I'm real
Fuck Who ain't feeling me

DMX taught me
How to pray,
through the ugly
Get up when I'm slippin'
There's beauty in the struggle

Drake taught me
It's cool to wear
my heart on a sleeve
And Cole said chase my dreams
Even when nobody believes

I'm a proud hip hop baby
My heart beats
in boom bap rhythms
808 bass
And my blood runs
In many flows

Slut-Shaming

I never thought
a woman was a hoe
For sleeping with me
On the first night,
Week,
Or
Month
To me,
It was actually
The highest compliment
If she was comfortable
Enough to be free with me
 in the most intimate way
Shortly after connecting
For the first time
I appreciated the decisiveness
And honesty

A woman's value
Was not measured By
how soon she slept me
Or how long she made me wait
It's funny
how some men
Get pissed at women
for making them wait
But call them sluts
When they fuck them
'Too early'

The Pisces

How does
that even make sense?

A weekend of pleasure
Became my happily ever after

If I had judged my fiancé for
Revealing herself too soon

My greatest blessing
would have
Slipped away

Michael Tavon

"You won't heal if you
 keep beating yourself up
over the things you can't change."

Realism

As soon I hear someone say
'be realistic'
I immediately tune them out.
I've made a living out of
redefining my reality,
I refuse to allow anyone
 to blur my vision with doubt.

Michael Tavon

"Distractions are like comfort food, the more you indulge, the less productive you become."

The Pisces

Note to Self:

When my heart is in the right place
 I will be able to make peace
with my decisions
when the outcome
doesn't go in my favor."

Michael Tavon

Dirty Internet Hobbies

It's the creative mind's
Greatest poison
I often find myself
Massaging my manhood
Like it's stressed after a long day,
Pleasuring myself
When I haven't done anything
To deserve the reward,
The afterguilt that
Swarms my mind
Like a gang of hornets
Stings when
I cum to my senses
I feel ashamed,
The amount of time and money
I invested
In my dirty internet hobbies
Could've been spent
On my craft,
I often wonder where
I'd be if I spent more time
Writing rather than
Doing meet and greets
with my Johnson
I'm embarrassed to admit
I've applied the 10,000-hour rule
To the wrong field
With my hands
Maybe, I indulge

The Pisces

In this dirty internet hobby
Because I'm afraid
Of my dreams
actually, coming true

Michael Tavon

Money Makes People Do Crazy Things

Like kill their spouse
To claim the life insurance policy
Or steal from the mother
To shop at Gucci

Money makes people do
Crazy things

Controlled by
a brittle sheet of paper
Printed with a face of
a dead white man

Money hungry people
are usually the saddest souls

Because having a lot
Is never enough

It's like a drug
They yearn for
More and more
And will do anything
To capture the high
They're chasing

To some money

The Pisces

is more important
than freedom

Funny, because money
Means nothing when you
die or rot in a cell

Michael Tavon

Too Much Judging, Not Enough Loving

Hawks don't shame
Dogs for not having wings
Cheetahs don't slander
Sloths for not having speed
Elephants don't kill
Mice for being small
Monkeys don't shoot
Giraffes for being tall
But humans
The 'sophisticated' species
Shoot
Hate
Fight
Berate
For
Having Different
Skin
Religions
Body types
Opinions
Hope is missing
Empathy is nonexistent
Animals are the superior
Kind in this kingdom

'PAC Taught Me

Heaven ain't hard to find
Shovel through dark times
To unveil my light

Believe in my
dreams
When the cloud
of self-doubt
Tries to shade my
parade
Never drown
when it rains

I'll shed so many
tears,
Keep my head up
Being soft don't
make me weak
this rose emerged
From concrete

Michael Tavon

Note to Self:

"Your heart will begin to beat softer once you stop pressuring yourself to live up to the expectations, they thrust upon you."

Politicians

They wear expensive suits
To feed pretty lies
to the poor and hopeful
Through their counterfeit smiles

~ then shuck and jive
For the black vote
Before pulling the rug of hope
From under their toes

Oh how they
dance around the truth
So gracefully
Like hippies at a bonfire
As they watch us burn
We burn so slow
So slowly we burn
At the mercy
Of their broken promises
Time and time again

Trusting a politician
Is like trusting a broken clock
You'll lose your sanity
Longing for Change

Michael Tavon

School Wasn't Made for Kids Like Me

Shaken out of a dream
To the sound of a screaming alarm,
As the sun rose to wake up its clouds,
my brainwaves, shocked
with anxiety rushing
Down my spine
As I hurried out of bed

Quickly, dressed
fueled my body,
With a pop tart
And cereal
Then traveled to school
The same morning routine
185 days a year,
For 13 years of my life
Like I was living in a boring
Episode of the twilight zone

Class was being
Stuffed inside a four-wall box
Along with twenty something strangers
separated by the boxes
We sat our bums in
For hours
we listened to
our teachers educate us on

The Pisces

how to think
Inside the box

So tired and bored
I often got in trouble
for dozing off
Or daydreaming

Teachers questioned
 If I had ADHD
Because I lacked focus.
Of course, the problem
Was me,
Not the outdated school system

We raised our hands
to speak
we needed permission
to use the bathroom
We did what we were told
Like the obedient pets
We were trained to be

Lunch, if you were
Poor like me,
ate for free
2% milk, cheap entree
And fruit juice
In a plastic tube
Only jails have worse
Food the public schools

When the day ended
I left feeling hollow

Like an organ donor's body

Now, as an adult
I loath my 9-5
Because working
Reminds me of school.
School only prepared kids like me
For jail or a job
They didn't teach us
How to dream

Fuck This Job

We are not our parents
Nor our Grandparents
Which is something to admire

We will take a job
But not die for it

We will take a job
to hold us over
But it won't let it
consume our lives

We'll say 'fuck this job"
And leave without notice
The moment
A 9-5 becomes detrimental
to our mental health
And move on to the next,
Older generations
Label us lazy
For playing musical chairs
With common jobs

They call us weak
For not sticking it out
When the job gets tough

What is so weak about knowing
 our worth?

Michael Tavon

What is so lazy about refusing
To be exploited?

We watched our parents
Trade their youth
For 20 years of misery
To receive minimum wage
As compensation for their
Dedication

We refuse to struggle
On billionaire's time
We'd rather do bad
On our own dime

Shotgun Love

Shotgun love,
You blast my heart
Then question
Why I'm falling apart

Shotgun love,
Tremors on my skin,
I beg for mercy
Before you pull the trigger,
Again

Shotgun love
My pain is a rush to you
The more I forgive
The more your lies
Come true

Shotgun love,
Shells killing me slowly
Dying next to you
Cuz I fear being lonely

Michael Tavon

Don't Be Cruel (lyrics)

(Hook)

Don't be cruel to my heart
Catch me when I fall girl
Don't be cruel to my heart
be down from the start

(Verse)

It's hard to repair
Trust once broken

You know this
So please don't leave
Me open and hopeless

I'd rather be guarded and lonely
And let fear control me
Than to let love
Get a hold of me
That was the old me

I'm telling you
To stay true
Or I'll turn our love
Into old news
Don't give me rain
When my sky is blue
Be my muse,
I'll paint you

The Pisces

In pretty hues

(Verse)
If your love
Is an ocean
Don't let me drown girl

If your love is the sky
Let me fly
don't shoot me down girl

Trust is my prized possession
What I'm stressing
If I give to you
Will you be a blessing
Or a lesson?

School of heartbreak
I graduated
 no more chasing
A love that ain't patient
I don't compete
I'm not racing
I'll get missing
Before
I waste my time racing
Against another man

Michael Tavon

Detaching Roots

As unforgettable you may be it is time to let you go. Detaching myself from the root of our memory is what I need to heal from the wreckage of the storm you caused. The more I fight against the fate of our demise, the less time we'll have to flourish. I'm infatuated by your essence, but we must move on to grow.

My First-First Love pt 1

My first heartbreak wore
Scars, lies, and short shorts
Like the latest fashion
And it fit her so well

Still wet behind the ears
I was everything she needed
 me to be

Lovable enough to fuck
And gullible enough fuck over

Held hostage by her secrets
She threatened to kill herself
Every time I tried to leave,

I was 17 and naive
She was 16 and well-seasoned
Like Thanksgiving collard greens

I thought we were twin flames
The way we fought and screwed
In the living room while
Her mother was at work

Every Friday
After school,
A new fight,

Michael Tavon

She couldn't stop fucking
Men twice her age
The thrill
was a drug to her

We would argue
Until her tears
Soaked the chest of my shirt
Then promised to never do it again,
Her short denim shorts
would hit the floor,
Our nude bodies too

She was my first happily ever after
Or I thought she was

"I'm fucking done,"
I said, after I learned
She screwed some boy in a stall.

She smiled and said she was
 2 months out of nine
A seed of mine
Growing inside
I cried, confused
The condom never popped

A week later
 she called
And said, "it's taken care of."

When I saw her mother
that Sunday,
She didn't mention a clinic

The Pisces

or abortion

They both had new
hair braided in
And a set of nails

By the look in her eyes
I Immediately knew,
It was a lie

I wasn't surprised since
Our home was built on a lie
Each wall holding on
For dear life

Then the ceiling collapsed
When the lie could no longer
Hold the infrastructure
Intact

Michael Tavon

The Forbidden Word

My mouth rattled like a serpent
As the poison spewed
 from my tongue

The word,
Was a force
That hit her
In the chest
Like a freight train

 a hundred sorry's
Couldn't repair the damage
As I watched her still,
Paralyzed

There's was no coming back
From what was said

That was the first and last
Time I called a woman
Bitch

My First- First Love pt 2

Remember when I said our home
Was built on a lie?

we met through Tasha,
Her older sister,
23, model type,
 baby daddy issues
My heart

I was drawn to her curly locks
And drama filled life
Tasha and I
Would flirt through
MySpace messages
And comments
She strummed the strings
Of my teenage heart,
Like a solo on Ed Sheeran's guitar
And the music felt damn good,

When she changed
her relationship status
To 'In a Relationship' with me
After a week
of sweet nothings,
We graduated
from MySpace notes
To falling asleep

Michael Tavon

on the phone
"I love you", she said
I returned
the affection she gave,
One night after
a fight with her baby daddy
She introduced me to her
Little sister
We laughed for hours,
Tasha insisted
I come to meet them

Their home was a fifteen-minute
Car ride away
So I hopped on my bike
And peddled
for 45 minutes
Under the summer sun
With a wrinkled condom
in my pocket
The little sister greeted
me at the door,
My shirt soaked
In sweat,
"Where's Tasha?"
I asked
"She left"
She smiled
She let me clean myself
up on the bathroom
Then We fucked in the swimming pool.

That was the beginning
of our relationship

The Pisces

The bike ride,
The wash-up,
The sex,
And me asking for Tasha.

After four months
I realized there was
no physical trace
Of Tasha or a baby
around their small apartment
Not even a picture
 in the living room
No mention of Tasha
or a grandbaby
From their mother

For every eyebrow raised
She had the perfect answers
To lessen my skepticism

Tasha and I
Kept in touch through
MySpace and the occasional
Three-way call with her sister

Tasha,
moved to Texas
with her baby daddy
To Never be heard from again

After 8 months
I ended the disaster
we called a romance
And I asked

Michael Tavon

"Is Tasha even real"

She stared with her wide
Froggy eyes
And said,
"it was me the whole time."

The Pisces

Chasing Your Dreams

I have a friend
Who's a fool for her
so bad
To the point
 it's literally killing him
The rotted teeth
From chain smoking
Cancer sticks,
Vacant spots on his head
Where hair once lived
They crossed his
receding hairline border
To find a new shore

He yearns for her so much
Some may mistake
His grandfather for a brother
Because she stole his youth

Every time she cheated
He formed his hand into a rock
And abused his wall
Every time she snuck around
He went hunting for her
With only her lies
For clues

They broke up

Michael Tavon

every pay period
And made up
every 5 business days
It was like a never-ending
Match of Tug of war
With one pulling away
to move on
And the other
refusing to let go

He wants her so much
He watched her fall in lust
With someone else
And remained her friend
Knowing it pained him every day

A beautiful baby,
Created by mistake
He didn't care it wasn't his
He continues to bend
over backwards
For her
Like he did a thousand yesterday's ago

When she became single
 His hope was reborn

She still treats him like a stray dog
But he enjoys the attention.

He told me
"I don't care she's what I want"

Despite being told

The Pisces

he is not the one
He still chases her like
the dream he will never catch

In a way this sick twisted
Passion inspires me

If he refuses
to give up on his dream
Why should I?

Michael Tavon

II

Rain & Dark Clouds

Dear Pisces V

You have a terrible habit of internalizing your pain. Once you express the feelings you buried deep into the depths of your heart, the boiling fire inside you erupts like a volcano. Your fear of conflict caused this implosion. One day I hope you stop letting your pain fester like an apple sliced open. Speak your piece to keep your peace, even if that means burning bridges you'll never cross again.

Michael Tavon

Stanger at Heart

Grains of sand trickle down
The hourglass of my tainted fate
taken for granted
Precious memories fade
Hours of regret
Days of Shame
Dying to hold
Onto raspberry dreams
While running from
Reality's blame

How does it feel
When father time
Doesn't give a damn you?

How does it feel
 when Mother Nature
Refuses to hug you?

How does it feel
When the water runs dry
And the flowers
 inside you gently die?

My crimson heart drums
A rhythm
I slowly pace to
Under the crescent moon
I would cry
If I die too soon
Left alone

The Pisces

On a dark noon
Forever with my shadow
And blinding hues

How does it feel
When you wanna live
But destined to die?

How does it feel
When you hold dreams
So close
But can't sleep at night?

How does it feel
When you yearn for warmth
But feel cold inside?

Michael Tavon

My Life is a Sad Song

It feels like my life is a series of sad songs playing on shuffle, and I can't help but sing along. I feel the pain crying from Prince's guitar strings as I dance under the pouring purple rain, with a flow of tears heavy enough to make levees break. Entrapped by sadness when I hear Cobain humming in my ear, something's in the way of my happiness, and I'm too numb to care. My heart breaks to Kanye's 808s as I try to survive the coldest winter of my life. My life is a sad song. I try to stay strong, then go back to black, as Amy sings me to sleep, I fall into a drunken stupor in this wine house. I could turn off the music or play happy songs, but I would be listening to a lie. My life is a sad song and I'll listen until it gets played out.

Tired of Being Tired

Darkness falls sooner
Than usual
And remains at play
For the sun to sleep in
It's so easy to lose track of time
When every hour looks the same
No amount of sleep
Can cure the weariness
my body feels
My mind has grown bored of
Things that used to entertain me
I've become a prisoner
in my own home

Work and grocery stores
Are the only places I go

I watch some of my peers
Travel without regard
And party without masks

Jealous of their ability
To rebel against the possibility
Spreading illness and death

Angry at their capacity
To not care for anyone's well being

Michael Tavon

Then there a people like me
Doing it the right way
Playing it safe
Work
Home
Work
Home
Protecting my health
While slowly losing my mind

darkness falls sooner
Than usual
I'm tired of being tired

Heartworking

My heart
Is the hardest
working employee
I know,

No smoke breaks,
No Sick Days
No PTOs,

He beats every moment
This precious life has to offer
Without a complaint

My heart
Enjoys working here
He tells me every day

I'm eternally grateful
To be blessed with
Such a hard-working heart
I'll never lose sight of that

My heart never wants
a raise or promotion

But one day he made

Michael Tavon

3 requests

1.stop worrying
about the future
2. Stop doubting myself
3. Show more gratitude

Because it would
make his job
 a hell of a lot easier
If I didn't create problems
By stressing over
things I can't control

Don't Wait 'Til I Die (lyrics)

(Hook)

Don't Wait Til I Die
To fucking love me

Don't wait til I'm gone
To want to hug me
Treat me like you want me
Don't treat me like
I'm nothing
Please
I swear to god
Don't wait til I die
to fucking love me

(Verse)
I really get high
Just To get by
Sometimes I stare at the sky
Breakdown and cry
This can't be life
This can't be life
When I go to my 9-5
It's like suicide

Michael Tavon

Cuz I'm killing myself
Dying inside
I don't wanna be rich
But I die trying
To stay afloat
After each paycheck
I start to lose hope
Like when's my day coming?
When will they love me?
When will they love me?
I'm chasing my dreams
A thousand miles and runnin
But I ain't going nowhere
Feels like I'm going nowhere
People say they love me
But do they really care?

(Verse 2)

(Sing)
I try to make peace with things
I can't control
I try to let go
But it's hard to move on
When feel it's like everything I
Do Is wrong

My mind spinning an axis
While I'm smoking In the dark
Bumping blackberry molasses
Feels like I only work
 just to pay taxes
Putting in these hours

The Pisces

Getting paid a fraction
What happening?
What's happening
People only support you
When you up or dead gone
I hope they choose to love
me after this song
I feel so lost
Where do I belong
Sometimes I feel so alone
In the worst way

30

As my twenties
Begin to pack their days
To say goodbye
I'm stuck between
Setting them free
And chasing after my
Wild youth -

Why am I hesitant to let go?
We've been through
 too much
For me the watch
them egress without a fight

The heartbreaks
Oh the many times I patched
My heart wounds
With 'So Sick' by Ne-Yo
I owe him a royalty check

The 1st Friday's,
And $2 drink, Monday's
Downtown
—-oh the nights
my heavenly temple
Was poisoned with ounces
Of The devil's juice
Lustfully grinding on
Women who wore dresses
Tighter than saran wrap

The Pisces

Hoping they felt
the joy in my pants
And would want to do
something about it

The sex-
Rocking the boat
With women
I wanted to care for
and women
I wouldn't trust
with my eyes closed
~ it was the thrill
Burning lust was
my adrenaline rush,
when my fix couldn't be fulfilled
I made fancy with my left hand
Until my wrist fell asleep

The self-loathing-
when sadness
Told me to stay in bed
Until the morning left
Or get high
until my cloudy mind
Got lost in yesterday
Or quit my
Deadend job
After my account over drafted
On payday
I swear,
going to the bank
Was more depressing than
A trip to the free clinic

Michael Tavon

Why would I not want
my twenties to move on?

When I smile
It's Still white as snow,
There's a gleam in my eyes
That makes the sun proud
When I inhale
My ribs no longer show-
I am healthier
than ever before,
Gray Wisdoms bloom
with the
coils of my hair
Love has found a home
in this body of mine

Why chase after
The years I've outgrown?

Maybe, shedding
who I used to be
Is scarier than
growing into someone
I'm unfamiliar with -

Love,
I'm transforming into love
And I'm proud
Of who I am becoming

Mountain Climb

It's an uphill battle
I continue climb
To find peace
On the other side
 My feet and hands swell
Under heat and pressure
I tap into my reserved strength
Despite harsh weather
knowing each stride
Brings me closer to paradise
Is why I keep my hope alive
I scratch
and claw my way
to the top
I refuse to stop
There is no quit
In my heart

Michael Tavon

<u>Sometimes it's Not as Loud as We Think</u>

My depression was a Library,
Comfy and silent
~ tone-deaf
To the violent
devastation inside me
Lost in my mind
No compass to
Guide me
Smiling, while gently
Falling apart
thoughts scattered
Like stars

My depression,
played the greatest trick
Of them all

my shell painted
With vibrant shades
To show signs of life
But the inside was a grave
I lived on the edge
To feel closer to death
A piss poor soul
Fooling myself
To be happy
When I needed Help

The Pisces

Comfort was the zone,
I never felt alone

Depression
made a home,
inside me

It was silent
Like mediation
Oblivious to the pain
I was escaping
Chasing the highs
To balance my lows
Coughing
from clouded lungs
Til I felt numb

Depression was a drug

Michael Tavon

Some days I feel like Cobain

Sometimes I wonder if fighting through the struggle is worth the trouble. What if the dark clouds inside me have no silver lining and the storms will consume my heart until I drown? The sun doesn't smile for me. Rainbows never glow in my direction and heartache is an earthquake that split my world in two. What should I do? I water my hope with tears, but the dry heat of disappointment keeps killing its chance to survive. In the end, I keep living, because I'm too stubborn to lose my battle with misery.

Something in the Way II

Like a fish
Flopping on the deck
I yearn for what I can't reach
Begging for mercy
As I wither away
To my listless fate
Void of feelings
I burn under the sun
Healing feels like a
Losing battle
before it has begun
Taken far from home
Lost in the air
Lack of hope
Suffocated my lungs
I'm desperate for a change
But change keeps
Slipping away

Michael Tavon

The Fantasy

Sometimes we fall
for the fantasy
of not being alone
So much
We force happily ever afters
Into temporary forevers,
Expecting happiness will bloom
From miserable soil

In My Feelings

Thoughts run deep like an ocean
But I can't float, I'm so hopeless
Now I'm drowning, can't focus
I try to leave my heart open
Then end up broken

Michael Tavon

Small Minds Think Alike

I dream in hues too vivid
For small-minded people
To comprehend

Small-minded people
offer Small-minded advice
From the dull realm
Of their small-minded reality

They often flock
by the dozens
like early birds,
To chirp cliches
In my ear
But I refuse to hear

Small-minded people
Loathe me
Because they don't fit the life
tailormade for me
So, they attempt to tear
the thread of my moral fabric
By deeming my dreams
Too unrealistic

I'd much rather have
the space to
Dream comfortably

The Pisces

Than be cluttered
By the thoughts
Of small-minded people

Sometimes being alone
just makes more sense

Michael Tavon

Stop sharing your dreams with small-minded people. They will only say things like "have a backup plan", "don't throw all your eggs in one basket", or "what if you don't make it? Your dreams won't grow if you're surrounded by clouds of doubt.

A Good Father is a Little Boy's First Best Friend.

I'm the son
Of a poe' man
But the son
of a loving man

The son of a man
Who played catch and hoops
With his boy after a twelve-hour
shift in the kitchen

The son of a man
Who taught his son patience
With fresh bait
And long talks
Over saltwater banks

The son of a man
Who watched sports with his son
Until dozing off into a beer coma
I watched the yeast
make his belly rise
Like baked bread
Over the years

The son of a man
Who played rounds of chess
With his son
And beat him every time

Michael Tavon

The son of a man
Who taught his son
How to sneak snacks
Behind mama's back

The son of man
Who tried to teach his son
how to swim
By tossing him
in the water,
Sometimes that's
The best way
To approach life

I'm the son of a poe' man
But a loving man
He never had a lot of money
But had a lot of time
He spent it on his baby boy

That boy didn't grow
up to be rich in cash
But he grew up to be
Wealthy at heart

My father was
my first best friend
And still is til this day

I Hate Moments Like These

You know
The moments when you feel fine
Then suddenly
Your heart
Starts pounding
Like a hounding landlord,
Your breath vacates your body
Leaving body hollow,
Confusion clouds your mind
As you wonder why
You feel suffocated
By your own thoughts

You feel weak for not
Having the strength
To carry the world
On your shoulders.

The walls suddenly
close in
til there is
nowhere to go

For reasons
Unsure
You feel alone

Anxiety,
Is the black sheep relative
Who visits unannounced
And sleeps on your couch

Michael Tavon

The Pisces

Nothing feels lonelier than being
an outsider in your own home,

You spend so much time
with your head in the clouds
The ground seems
too shaky to step on

You dream in color
'Cause reality is grey and white
So, you reside inside the paradise
You designed in your mind

Cause
Nothing feels lonelier than being
an outsider in your own home,

You wear your heart
On a sleeve
Despite the world being cold
Your youth was tainted,
Somehow you remained gold

ugly thoughts often
Travel through
Your beautiful mind
Lost between

The Pisces

Dark and light
Someday you'll realize
Heaven ain't hard to find
Even when
Nothing feels
lonelier than being
alone in your own home,

Michael Tavon

Color Me Crazy

When my mood turns bluer
Than Chicago's night skyline
And all red hell burns behind
My white smile
Will you gaze into my brown eyes,
And say everything will be fine?

When thoughts darker than
The deepest depths
 of the Arctic Ocean
Rush to the surface
Of my grey-pink mind
Will you embrace my brown skin
 with heavenly openness
To help me feel less hopeless?

It's not your job to save me,
But when sorrow comes to use
My body as a canvass
Will you color me crazy
Or paint some soft bright hues
On my dark weary heart?

I need to know,
Before I let my walls
Down, for you

Happiness

It may come and go
Like distant kin
Be sure to
Treasure the time spent
Because you'll never know
the next time you'll feel it again.

Michael Tavon

Mind Storms

When the thunder
in your heart roars
and the clouds inside
your mind begins to pour,
remember there are rainbows
in your soul,
Eager to glow

This storm is a breakthrough
To a new beginning

Twilight

As Twilight joy
Shines through
My clouded darkness
I capture this Kodak moment
With my crystal iris lens
Knowing this feeling
Won't last forever
But the thought of
Making this moment last forever
Is comforting enough

Michael Tavon

Smile more

Your smile has the force
 to tear down
the walls other's built
around their hearts.

Your smile has the gift
of creating a harmony
infectious enough
To make laughter a song

Your smile can
Sow wounds
and heal scars

Your smile
is the sun that shines
After the storm
To assure you're not alone

Your smile has the courage
To fight against fear

Your smile has enough influence
To change a stranger's day
~~
Your smile has the magic
To make someone's
Angst disappear

The Pisces

A smile
 is the universal sign
For caring

So, smile
Don't hold back
From sharing

Michael Tavon

I Haven't Cried in a Long Time

I don't know if it's a good
Or bad thing
Does it mean
I'm free from yesterday's harm
Or am I containing my rage
Like heat in a can

I haven't cried in a long time
Is that a sign
For better days
Or am I overdue for a cleanse

I have cried in a long time
I wonder why,
Confusion fogs my brain

I'm supposed to be happy
My eyes haven't rained
In many days

But all I can think
Is what's going to cause
The storm inside me
To pour again.

III

Star Gazing

Dear Pisces IV

You can be unstable like the waters your tread. There's no shame in the emotional depth you carry, you just need an anchor to keep you from drowning. Some days it's hard to navigate through the waves of your moods all alone, so don't push away the people you love when they offer and helping hand. It's okay to receive help. You can't be the one doing all the saving.

Dear Rain

The way you flow from the sky with such grace and land on the surface, glistening like diamonds amid sunlight puts my heart at ease and mind on autopilot. You're mother nature's favorite song when pellets of you drum windows and windshields. I feel so in tune with your melody; you send chills running down my spine the way Phil Collins does when he sings "in the air tonight". When you're in the air at night, bliss rains from my eyes. I feel my fears shedding as you shower my skin with gentle forgiveness. I embrace you when you're calm and infatuated with your rage. I know when to reciprocate your affection and when to give you space. You and I share the ideal friendship. When I immerse myself in your shower, you never let me drown, and when I'm caught in awe by your beauty you wash me off my feet. A sight to behold, a mystery my mind tries to unravel. My shower from heaven. My heavenly shower

Michael Tavon

My Dear Nightfall

Some nights you're
warm and soothing
like the voice
of Jhene Aiko
as I cocoon myself in a
blanket until I evolve
as a lively butterfly
when the sun smiles
through my window.
I blissfully dream
when you protect me
from the horrors of
the outside world.

Other nights you haunt me like regret and cage
me in. As ever-present you are, I often feel more
alone when you arrive. There's nowhere for me
to hide. My nightmares feel so surreal when you
decide to fuel my anxiety with more doubts

My Dear Darkness

You bring peace
and
sorrow to my soul

When daylight goes home
And you come outside
I must mentally prepare
For whatever mood you're in

You possess the power to
Keep me alive
or slowly kill me

My dear darkness
How I admire and despise
you

Michael Tavon

Saltwater Paradise II

I miss,

the sting
Of saltwater in my eyes,
Feet sinking into
The wet bed
Like quicksand

the unfiltered heat
Burning my brown skin
Like ants under
A magnifying glass

Day drinking
With good strangers
Who became best friends
For three hours

the music loud,
Volleyball matches,
Pretty clouds
Free-spirited women,
Nature sounds

I ain't the best swimmer
But the ocean always
Feels like home

The Pisces

It's the one place
We all go to feel less alone

The beach
Is the most
Liberating place
In the world

We take
off our masks
And flaunt
who we truly are

Michael Tavon

This May Sound Cocky but...

The funniest thing
About being an artist
Are the losers
Who claim they can do better
But never will
The idiots who don't possess
An ounce of my talent
But judge my entire
Body of work
Off one piece,
And the naysayers who can't
Even dream of doing
What I've already accomplished
Trying to convince me to quit,
delusions of grandeur
flood their minds
Jealously settles
In their bitter hearts
Deep down inside
It kills them
To see someone
Living the dream
they can't have
So, in their pathetic attempt
To shoot me down
They fail to realize
My confidence is bulletproof
Their negativity won't penetrate

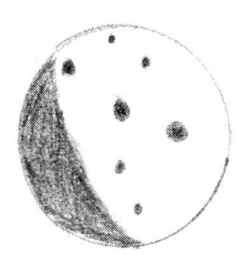

Sweet Dreams

Clouds blanket my pain
I surrender to the moon
Sweet Dreams in the sky

Michael Tavon

Two Week Notice

Today I begin a new life,
A life without the burden -
The burden of being controlled,
        Controlled by the false security
        Of a dull reality
    A dull reality
   where hope goes to die

Today I begin a new life
  A new life of thrill
 The thrill of seeing my dream
Manifest into a reality
Before my bright eyes
My bright eyes,
  will cry happy tears

Today I begin a new life
      A new life,
I'm turning in my two-week notice
My two-week notice,
  signed goodbye
  Goodbye to the old life
  The old life,
     I've fought so hard
    To move on from

<u>Escape</u>

Once I stopped
trying to escape
The healing
I was finally able
to fully embrace
The truth
I was I trying to elude

Michael Tavon

Clarity

Drippings from the sky
Washing away my regrets
I see clearly now

"You don't have rain on my parade when I'm celebrating myself; it's possible to be happy for me while wanting more for yourself too."

Michael Tavon

What's Yours is Mine

Your joy is my joy
Your pain is my pain

Your sun is my sun
Your rain is my rain

Your cool is my cool
Your stress is my stress

Your failure is my failure
Your success is my success

My dear friend
My kindred soul

From the heart
You will never be alone

Through summer madness
And winter bliss

Through heartaches
And wedding kisses

I'll be there,
I'll be there

The Pisces

To be everything
You need me to be

As long as your energy
Doesn't Drain or degrade me

Michael Tavon

Sorry I Was a Deadbeat Friend

Sorry
 I went missing
Like a child
on the back
 of a milk carton
Without rhyme or reason,

Sorry,
I vanished
For
weeks,
Months,
Years
Without sending
a text
Tweet
Or postcard,
I am a deadbeat friend
I admit
A deadbeat friend

I'm sorry
I turned down
every invite,
To hang out
The way
Young souls do

The Pisces

But my sadness
had better plans

I was afraid to hang out
Because when the
Inevitable
"How have you been"
Gets asked.

"Burying myself in self-loathing
While trying to find comfort
in the dark
and Feeling more worthless
than a counterfeit dollar bill.
 Inside my mind,
performing magic tricks
with my emotions.
I've been meaning
to get back to you,
but my depression
been so heavy
it's hard to carry myself
out of bed each morning."
Is what I would
want to tell you.
Instead,
"Just chillin'"
Is what you
Would hear
From me

I'm sorry
I was a dead friend
It wasn't you;

Michael Tavon

it was me
I didn't want your sunshine
To be swallowed
by my hurricanes

My overthinking
Created a life
Without you
And I saw you were
Better off without me

I know friends
Are supposed to give friends
A chance to be there for them

I know friends
Are supposed to vent
to friends when they
Need someone to talk to

I'm sorry
I was a dead beat friend
I tried to erase you
As if our friendship
Was written in pencil

You deserved better
I hope you give me
a second chance

The Pisces

Now, when you ask
"How have you been"
I'll say
"Just fine"

This time
It will be the truth

Diary

Your secrets will be locked safe
With me from the moment
They travel from your lips
To my mind

I'm your most loyal soldier
In the war of fear and heartache
I will die with
the most intimate details
Of your existence
Engraved in my brain

Your secrets,
Become mine,

Letting your guard down,
exposing me to your
Naked soul
Is an honor
I won't break

Honestly,
by the time
You summon the courage
To thrust your darkness
into the light
My intuition
Already knew the truth

The Pisces

As a dear friend
Your secrets
Will never become ammo
If war ever wage between us
Your secrets
Will never become blackmail
To keep you close to me

If our friendship
Falls from the peak
Of our mountain top
Your secrets
Will die with me

As Alicia Keys once
Said "Just think of me
as the pages in your diary"

Michael Tavon

<u>Deep</u>

How deep is your love
Open wide guide me inside
I'll get lost in you

Fast Car, Slow Life

My father's car
Was rusty & grey
When the engine cranked
The sound of a bursting
shotgun cracked the air
A trail of dark grey exhaust
Polluted the air
As he drove
'Roun the block

"We can smell yo daddy
coming from a mile"
The neighborhood kids
made jokes.

Momma often rode
 the city bus to work
The neighborhood kids
mocked that too

Our life was a game
 of musical chairs
Moving from house to house
Neighborhood to neighborhood
Feeling out of place

Michael Tavon

Felt normal to us

Money never flowed
Money was made
at the minimum
Between the two

Pops chugged
Beer after beer
Like a frat boy

Momma switched
the home decor
more than her
hot n cold moods,

People saw our life
as a punchline
But we were not laughing

Through the shortcoming
And sadness
My parents
Made sure their children were
Safe and happy

This is why I never realized
How poor were until
I started working

From Me to The Universe

However long this moment may last, I will bask in this blessing with electricity flowing through my veins. Not a single day will be taken for granted, nor will I become complacent in my present space. I will continue to reach higher than the mountains I've already climbed. With 20/20 vision I will never lose sight of the way paved for me. I'm eternally grateful you chose me to be your vessel. I promise to never disappoint you.

Michael Tavon

IV:

Constellations & Everything in Between

Heaven Sent

With flesh as soft as angel skin
I feel the bliss
In your tenderness
When we close our eyelids
And we slow dance in
Each other's dreams

Michael Tavon

I Knew Heaven Was Real II

I knew Heaven was real
The moment you said
you loved me
cause love dragged me
through hell
so many times
my heart became numb
to the flames
But when you said 'I love you'
A sensation rushed
 through my aorta
And I no longer
Felt alone in a crowded room
To you,
Love wasn't a fairytale
Nor a crutch
For your pain
Or a coping mechanism
For your trauma
Love was your godly
Essence
A treasure you were eager
to bless me with
For the first time,
Love didn't feel like a chore,
sweepstakes, or contest.
You appreciated
My soul and flesh
You didn't treat my love language

The Pisces

Like a foreign tongue
You listened to the beat
of my heart
As it carried a new tune
You danced to the melody

Michael Tavon

Poetic Justice

My poetic justice
Our word is bond
Like gorilla glue
Our poems will survive
through any storm

But I vow to never put your
Heart through
hurricanes and blizzards
My love is like hot chocolate
In the winter
Hit the spot
With every sip
Deep warm pleasure
Sizzling On your lips
When we kiss
I reminisce on the life
I had before you arrived
And wonder how I survived

It's funny,
You loved me
Before I had money
And living in mom's garage

You fell for the real
 me, no mirage

In return, you showed
your true colors

The Pisces

No disguise
Your heart,
Shines in vivid hues
Like northern lights in the sky

My summer sun
In July
Hot and filled with passion
Baby, you're
Everything I asked god for
You're magic

Michael Tavon

Magic Love

You believe in me
Because I never lie to you
I will not repeat
The harm other lovers
Caused to you

Our souls gravitated
to each other fast
But paced at the speed
Our hearts raced
For each other
So, nothing was forced
You're my twin flame
And our fire was torched
Symbol is forever
No divorce
You're everything
I was searching for
And more

My lady
You are magic

<u>Starlight (rap verse)</u>

You're a poem in the flesh
Your heart beats in riddles
Metaphors I can't get
You speak in rhythms
Physic dreams, I envision
When you're distant
Sonic passions, in the wind
I hope you listen
Like starlight
Your smile glistens
When you whisper
Psychedelic eyes
My mind trippin'
Love on the water
And rocks skippin'
hope I land
Before reality pinches

I know the feeling hurts
You're such a flirt
Running through
Strawberry fields
In sunflower skirts
Losing you would be the worse

But I guess you don't mind
for you it ain't hard to find
As time flies
I hate goodbyes
Dark nights and silent Cries

Michael Tavon

(Hook)
Do you dream
with your eyes open?
Do you sleep when wide awake
it's hard when you're alone
Please don't break

I wish I were a starlight
So, you could wish upon
The sky
I wish I were a starlight
So you could
see me every night

Simplicity

To the outside world
We had nothing tangible
To celebrate our soul tie,
In actuality
We shared an entire
Universe between us
Which was more than enough

Michael Tavon

Wanting you from a distance

As our souls' slow dance
In a Celestial realm
My heart aches
When it beats for your touch
Because our physical beings
Are distant
like childhood memories,
When Pleasant thoughts of you
Traverse the waves of my mind
I take a voyage to Atlantis
To feel you close to me,
Suddenly
reality pays a visit
To remind me
That we admire our hearts
Ten thousand miles apart
But I'll always come back to you
There isn't a mountain
High enough to keep me away
From you
Even though our bodies
Are oceans away
Our hearts,
Remain connected
I rest at ease
Knowing our bond is protected
By the moon
My dear,
I'm so eager to feel
Your breath gently exhale
on my chest hairs

The Pisces

Like winter wind
on autumn leaves
I miss you,
I miss you
I'm so happy
we found each-other
Despite the distance
I can't wait to kill
Space between us
And spend a lifetime
Hand in hand

Sincerely,
Yours truly

Michael Tavon

Goofballs

Echoes of our laughter
Floats through the still of darkness
As we tell inside jokes
And recite our favorite quotes
From Film and television shows
Not a single moment is dull,
It's a pleasure to know
Such simplistic joy
Lives in our home

New Love, New Places

After "Acura Intergurl by Frank Ocean"

I'm from palm trees
Skin tanning heat
Cloud showers
Beach Waves
Sandy feet
Hurricanes
And reptiles

But when I met you
I became
Mountains
snowstorms,
Orange leaves,
Small towns
Deer, foxes
And silent roads

I'm a long way from
the home
I was born
But I found
a new one in you,
With you

I kiss you
With the promise
Of 100 thousand tomorrow's

Michael Tavon

Even when my ashes
Drift into the sky
I'll refuse to say goodbye

My flame for you
will Never die
Never die

We Should've Stayed Friends

We were so eager
To fall head over heels
For each other
That We lost balance
Between desire and reality

Dazed and confused
Between the blurred lines
Of romance
We tricked ourselves
Into believing
Our friendship would bloom
Into bride and groom
Over time
Your body began
to speak a language different
From your words
And I became deaf to the truth

You wanted me
I wanted you too
In the end
We discovered
Our 'I love you's'
Had different point of views

Michael Tavon

In the end
We Both regretted
What we did
Too bad we could
Never return as friends

Shadow Dancers

…And then
we kissed at midnight
As we watched
our shadows slow dance
Amid the twilight.

Michael Tavon

A Funny Love Story

After a few months
Of friendship,
Flirting,
and being dirty on FaceTime
She took a flight
From Connecticut to Florida
She texted me when
her flight landed
I rode the bus downtown
There was an earthquake
In my stomach,
I wore black pants,
A black sweater,
And black shoes
Amid the heat of summer
I planned this grand introduction
In my mind, upon her arrival
Like the perfect scene from
A cheesy Romance
The plan was to meet her
Outside of the hotel
She would jump
Into my arms
And we'd kiss
Until we could taste
What we had for breakfast,
Then I'd carry her to the room
Toss her onto the bed
And practice making babies.

The Pisces

"I'm five minutes
away she texted me"
The hotel was ten minutes away
And I had to foot it,
7 minutes in
Sweat began to drip
From my pits
And forehead
The scent from my balls
Made me consider going
 Back home,
Two honks from a horn
 Made me gaze to the roadside
It was her motioning me
To climb inside
The rental car,
As I did
A silence as cold
As ice,
Froze time,
All I could think about
Were my sweat soaked clothes
And how our first weekend
Would be out last
"There's no way she's
 Gonna come back"

Michael Tavon

I said to myself
But the moment
We walked entered the hotel room
She jumped into my arms
And kissed me so deeply
I could've drowned
That weekend,
Our happily ever after began

Coordinates

Our hearts,
Engraved with the coordinates
Of where our souls reconnected
So no matter
How far we travel
We will never feel lost,
again

Michael Tavon

Forget About Him (Lyrics)

(Hook)

Girl I know what he did
But I ain't who he is
If you give me the chance
you'll forget about him

(Verse)

 u wanna
forget the past, girl
You thought life
With him would last, girl
You took flight
Then you crashed, girl
Now he got
Going out sad girl

He didn't love real you
Time to leave his ass
in the rearview
To see your real love
In clear view
Let get near yo

I wanna float

The Pisces

Rise high with you
So high
On a cloud
In the sky
With you
I'll never wanna
come down with you

I'm here
when you're Ready
No rush,
Go steady
Your heart is heavy
From the burdened you carry

So focus on you
But I'll be there
My friend
If you ever fall
In love again.

Michael Tavon

All Your Luv { Lyrics },

Your heart's been broken
Time and time again

All you need is an intimate friend
whose down for you
Til the very end

I swear

I'll love you naturally
Be as real as the sea

You won't hear lies from me
I swear

I'll be nothing less
Than what's best for you
I'll never settle
 for anything less than you
I swear

Your vibe is right
One of a kind
I ain't gonna do anything
To dim your shine

I swear

The Pisces

(Hook)

All your love is mine
Til the end of time
All I need is
you in my life
I swear

All your love
is safe with me
Treat me like a diary
You love is mine
To keep

I swear

(Verse 2)

can't get you the world
But i can give all of me
No expensive rings
But my heart
Ain't cheap

I swear

I'll give a love so fly
A rich man would cry
Because he still won't have
You by his side

I swear

Michael Tavon

I may be broke
But I won't break your heart
As long
As you play your part
I'll give you my all

I swear

Are you ready
For this journey, baby
Cause it ain't easy

Before we go
let me know

I swear

About a Girl 3 (lyrics)

Being lonely ain't fun
 I was Cupid's fool

I was too far gone
Then came you

I wasn't looking at all
You came out the blue
And show me
A feeling So neW

(Pre bridge)
I told her

If I fall in love again,
you will be my friend
Til the end

Bridge)
(Then she said:)

Baby, if you want me
Come have me
I ain't wasting yo time

Come fuck me
Like you love me

Michael Tavon

Come hold me
Like you want me
You won't feel lonely
lonely Again.

(Verse 2)

fuck the lonely out of me
(Lonely out me)
I'll stroke yo pain away,

No need to worry
I'll be yo one and only

If i give you my all
Will catch me
When I fall
in love
With you
Let know
Before I do

(Pre-bridge)
If you Give TLC
I vow not to creep around
wasn't looking for
Love, but it was still found

(Bridge)
(Then she said:)

Baby, if you want me
Come have me

The Pisces

I ain't wasting yo time

Come fuck me
Like you love me
Come hold me
Like you want me
You won't feel lonely
 lonely Again.

Michael Tavon

Student of Love

Our parents
Never taught
us how to love
Neither did school

Ain't no course
curriculum
Or syllabus
To learn
About the
most important course
Of our lives

All we have is films
And fiction
To romanticize

 - when they set us free
into the wild
On the hunt for love
We're like chicken
With heads cutoff,
aimlessly wandering
Hoping to stumble upon
The type connections
 we romanticized in
'The Notebook"
'Love & Basketball'
"Twilight"

"Love Jones"

They never taught us
how to maintain
honest relationships
So, we fail
~ hard and often ~
Until our hearts harden
And we hide behind a wall
Made of bricks
And trust issues

We were never
taught how to love -
Or trust it all together
By the time true love
presents itself
We're too
exhausted
and guarded
To try again

Michael Tavon

I Knew Heaven Was Real II

Darling, I know
You're used to love
Being a raging war
between colliding hearts
That eventually leads to casualties
And breaking a part
But you and I
Will only rise higher
I aspire to inspire
You in the right ways possible
Because I admire
The dark clouds
and sunshine inside you
I'm fascinated by your storms
And moonlight too
Your whole being is beautiful
Come close to me
For a love
people commonly dream of
But rarely attain
I'll never leave like Bobby Brown,
New Edition
I can stand the rain
I'm no doctor
But let me ease the pain

I knew Heaven was real
when you said you loved me
I hope you feel the same
When I say it too

Anchor

The weight of grief
Will never anchor you down
as long as
My arms are strong enough
To keep you away from
darkness

Michael Tavon

Mood Lights

Turn the lights down low
Tell me what you feel
Turn the lights down low
Tell me what you hear

I don't need to see
when I hear your body
 Calling for me,
Sexual telepathy

Let's play a game

I'll Switch the lights
To different hues,
And Do what I tell you to

Submit to me baby,

When the room turns violet
We entangle
In soft gentle violence
Until our breathes turn silent

When we see the color
That remind us of oceans
We'll rock steady
Deep strokin' and moanin'
In slow nothin'

Switch the pace
When red fills the space

The Pisces

Let out our burning desires
Set the sheets ablaze

Until we reach
Our climax

No matter the color
We create our own hue
When making
art to each other

Michael Tavon

The Bees

When my lips land
on your flower
My tongue
gets addicted to your nectar
Your sweet honey land
Brings my body infinite pleasure

Your womb is the nest
I rest my own body,
Feasting off honeycombs,
You wonder why I'm a homebody

You're my summer heat
and spring shower
the perfect match
Like bees and flowers

Skydiving hearts

Falling in love
with a soul
Who was once a stranger
Feels like skydiving
The rush of
Clouds hugging your body
As you gracefully
Descend amid the wind
Carried by adrenaline
Void of fear,
The thrill feels good
Until the ground is near
And reality punches your gut,
You see there's only
two ways it could end
A smooth landing
Or a disastrous crash
Falling in love
Is an extreme sport
That may kill you
Or make you feel more alive

Michael Tavon

P.s. I love you

When my soul
Finds a new home
Use these words
To help your mind feel whole
When your body feels alone

Don't dwell in my demise,
As time goes by
my love will be immortalized
By the letters I write
I hope you Smile, sometimes

By your side
I will always be
Even when I die
You'll never lose me
From love spells cast in ink
A love bonded for eternity

Lo(Falling)Ve

The feeling never tells you when it's on the way. It never shoots any warning flares in the air. Nor does it ask to come into your life but suddenly arrives as a pleasant surprise and gives you the ride of your life. Love can be so inconsiderate, but does what it has to do, knowing most people would scurry away like a wild rabbit, if they knew love was on the way.

Michael Tavon

Sex Olympics

She calls me
Mr. all-nighter
Cause I go round for round
Like a prizefighter

She enjoys when
I fold her legs like a pretzel
In the sheets
When we wrestle

Fucking is a sport
A sight to behold
If sex were the Olympics
We'd be going for gold

You Make Love Feel Easy

Falling deeply into depths of you
Feels like a gentle dive
into friendly waters
Even though
I can't swim
in deep waters
I trust
you won't let me drown

You make love feel so easy
There's no struggle between
Our beating hearts
Every day with you feels
like Sunday morning

Michael Tavon

Be Longing

For so long
I longed for someone
Who longed for me
As much as I longed for them

Love Language II

She prefers the type
of gifts that says
I remember obscure
references from her favorite
romance films
Or handwritten
Notes spilling out
my deepest feelings
in ink form
Or a Memento
That reminds her of childhood joy
Yes, diamonds are gorgeous
But nothing says
'I love you'
More than a gift
That makes her smile
And say
"I can't believe you remembered"

~ Effort impresses
her more than diamonds

Michael Tavon

The Pussy Fairy

My dear,

hypnotize me with the spell
between your thighs
mile high loving
Make me never wanna
to come down

Entrap me with the magic
Of your passion
I'll be passive
And do what you ask of me

Get me drunk off lust,
Intoxicate me
With your touch
Quench my thirst
Put it on my tongue

My personal pussy fairy
Put it on me daily
Your supernatural love,
Leaves my soul shaking

Love Language I

Extravagant gifts may
please the eyes
For a few moons and suns
But it's the small gestures,
You do
That aligns the stars in my heart
To form constellations
vivid enough to shine
Beyond the end of time
For you

Michael Tavon

Never Lie

From the depth in her stare
My heart feels secure knowing
A lie has never traveled past
Her promising lips

The Unicorn

She was something
I wasn't used to
something
My heart was unfamiliar with

She was beyond the usual
Far from my type,

She was rare,
Like a bismuth crystal
With the allure of
A calming waterfall

She was wild
Like a unicorn
Galivanting across the plane
But unlike women before her
I didn't have to chase
To prove my worth
she was ready to
Share her wild heart with me

Michael Tavon

Faith

Dying is easier than living
and each breath we inhale
Is us exercising the choice
To remain alive

With a million ways to die
And only a few ways to live
There's something inside us all
That gives us the strength to keep
Battling our demons

a great deal of luck
And a special dose of faith
Is needed
To make it as far as we have

For the times we consider
Ending it all
There's a voice in our Head
telling us
Better tomorrow's will come

faith is the fuel
That keeps us going

Longing to give up
is not a weakness
It's a sign
That it's time
To show your heart
some mercy & forgiveness

The Pisces

Dying is was easier than living
But it's best to
Find the meaning behind
The suffering
Because The joy will be more fruitful
Once you understand why

So live my friend
Don't end your life

Michael Tavon

Regular People are Special

It's the carriers
Who trudge through
heavy snow
To deliver the news
We depend on

It's the nurses
Fueled by coffee
And energy drinks
To show hero's
Don't need capes to save us

It's the restaurant server
Sacrificing their holidays
 To help ungrateful guests

It's the everyday people
not rich, nor famous
Who keeps the world spinning

The Pisces

Rest In Peace II

Rest in Peace
 to the former me,
I must lay you to rest
so I can create the
space to
grow into the best
version of myself
I hope you understand

Michael Tavon

Birthdays

"Happy birthday cheers"
made me feel
Closer to my expiration date,
Every time I blew out the candles
On my cake
I loathed growing closer to death
And further away from joy

The 'you're getting old jokes'
On hallmark cards
Were reminders
That I was
running
out of time

I often tried
To dodge
celebrations
Like they were
bill collectors
'Cause aging
under the sun
Was never fun
To me

The Pisces

It took a while
To realize how much
Of a blessing it is
To survive 365 days a year

Each moment is precious
Life is fragile

Once I stopped
Viewing birthdays
as a death curse
I began to see birthdays
as a symbol
Of growth

Now I'm eager
To embrace the journey
Of growing old

Michael Tavon

Cheetahs have Anxiety Like Me

Society terrorizes
 The weak
The shy
The sensitive
The quiet
The outnumbered
Just like animals in the wild.

Sometimes life
is too much to handle.
Even for the fastest
creature on land
No matter how fast they run
Trouble seems
to be around the corner

I feel the same way
The world continues
to beat me down
Then question
my fear of getting harmed

They Say Never Question God

So unfair
So many mysteries
Left unanswered,
I'm itching to understand
As fingers rake through my hair
As I try to organize my confusion

Why can't I question the one
who has all the answers?

Why can't I doubt what God does
When so much doesn't make sense

Why did Kobe die?
When will the black nation finally
See the light at the end
of this never ending
Dark tunnel?
What's the meaning behind
all of our suffering?
What happens after we die?

So many questions, unanswered

Life is the most complicated
Equation,

Michael Tavon

We know x equals death,
but we spend our
Dwindling time
 trying to figure out
The rest in between

We can't ask for help
We can't question God
We can't ask if it's a man or woman
Moon or sun
We can't disagree with what's done

So, what's the point of it all,
Living
Being alive

We're Tied by the strings
Of this merciless puppet master
And there's nothing
We can do to change our fate

Celebrities Don't Make Decisions for me

I am my own mind
My thoughts aren't swayed
By what strangers think

My heart beats to a tune
Too unique to copy and paste
Any other melody

Celebrities don't
make decisions for me
I don't follow what they believe
They aren't Gods
And what they preach isn't gospel

I admire their art,
Not the mirage they
Call their lives

When people ask
How could I support Kanye
How could I support Lil Wayne.
'Cause they endorse Trump

I say I enjoy their music
I don't give a shit
About their political affiliations
Personal affairs
Or preferences

art is the only thing that matters
the gossip is irrelevant to me

Michael Tavon

Trends I don't follow
Celebrities are humans
And all humans say stupid things
That's why I will never
 Look to a famous person
To make decisions for me

I Didn't Say I love You to Hear it Back

I want you to know
how I feel
Even if you don't feel
the same
Or too afraid
to let down your guard
Because being vulnerable
is a death sentence to you
I love you
Even if you don't say it back

How I feel about you
Won't break
Because of the words
You don't say

Michael Tavon

Broken Records

Some friends fade
Like the end of songs

The tune can be replayed
But the feeling
Will never be the same

The fun
The love
The rush
All lost,
~ Slips away

Some friends
are meant to be enjoyed
For a few seasons
Just like good songs

Once you outgrow the song
Or the song outgrows you
You must say goodbye,
Spare the bitter feelings,

Because
The connection you hold
Near and dear
No longer exists
In the present

Sometimes nostalgia
Will trick us into spinning
Broken records

The Pisces

With hopes
Of recapturing
Feelings once shared
With friends
Who faded away
Seasons ago

Michael Tavon

The Herd

This country isn't designed
To support bravery,

Hatred is the spoken language
Of the native tongue, here
Love is foreign, here

The facades wear masks
Disguised as honesty

This country isn't designed
To support courage

stand up
for what you believe in,
They call you a liar
For not falling
For anything.

Pursue your passion,
They call you insane
 For dreaming

Follow your heart
They'll call you lost
For not being a happy
Sheep amongst the herd

Before I die
I hope they call me

The Pisces

the craziest, most dishonest,
and loneliest
Motherfucker to ever live

Because I refused
to learn the language
They tried to force
me to speak

Michael Tavon

Boys in the Hood

Boys will be boys
We didn't know any better
Our inquiring minds
Explored the shoeboxes
Hidden under our cousin's bed
And discovered more
than condoms
And mixtapes

We were warned not to taste
The residue on the counter
'Cause it's the dangerous
kind of sugar

Boys will be boys
When we're bored
With no place to go
So we found ourselves
In spaces we didn't belong

We picked up bullet shells
From the ground
And jam them
In nerf guns
Running' round the yard,
Pretending to be the cops
That would eventually
try to kill us
And the robbers
Some of us became

The Pisces

Because it's one
Of the few career paths
We had to choose from
--
As boyz in the hood
there are few places
to go to keep
out of trouble

Because of budget cuts
And gentrifiers,
Many boys are forced to find
Their fun in the streets
Where trouble is only
Around the block

Cardinal Songs

I once loathed the sound
of cardinals singing
good morning tunes
to wake me
out of my dreams,
so ungrateful
of me
to not appreciate
the most pleasant
reminder
of being blessed to
see another sun

Light Inside Me

As a child
I would form a telescope
with of my hand
and trace
my own constellations
in the night sky
until my eyelids
felt heavy

On summer noons
I spent hours molding
clay sculptures out of clouds
until the sun
burnt my palms

Some days,
grandma's dirt coated lawn
would be my canvass,
as I used
loose sticks
to paint pictures
from my wild imagination
until filth
rose up my shins
like fire smoke

Michael Tavon

Looking back now,
I was born to create
Before I knew my purpose
The child in me still resides
In this adult body
Of mine
My creative light
Will shine
'til the day I die

The Exit

When I leave
Let it be like
A whisper in the dark

I don't wish to go out
Loud and bright
Like fireworks

Fireworks,
are often forgotten
After they fade
off into the clouds

my departure
Shall be gentle, subtle

Let the memory
Of my presence
Linger in the hearts
I've touched,
The minds
I've crossed

Remember me,
Allow my essence
To pleasantly haunt
This place
Like a whisper in the dark

Michael Tavon

Dear readers,

Instead of calling it **The End**
Let's say 'I love you,
and I hope to hear from you soon.'
Thanks for growing with me